TEEN SURVIVAL GUIDE

SURVIVING GYM CLASS

JOHN A. TORRES

Enslow Publishing
101 W. 23rd Street
Suite 240
New York, NY 10011
USA
enslow.com

Published in 2018 by Enslow Publishing, LLC.
101 W. 23rd Street, Suite 240, New York, NY 10011

Library of Congress Cataloging-in-Publication Data

Names: Torres, John Albert, author.
Title: Surviving gym class / by John A. Torres.
Description: New York : Enslow, 2018. | Series: Teen survival guide | Includes bibliographical references and index. | Audience: Grades 7–12.
Identifiers: LCCN 2017016540| ISBN 9780766091900 (library bound) | ISBN 9780766093591 (pbk.) | ISBN 9780766093607 (6 pack)
Subjects: LCSH: Physical education for children—Juvenile literature. | Physical fitness—Juvenile literature.
Classification: LCC GV362 .T67 2018 | DDC 372.86—dc23
LC record available at https://lccn.loc.gov/2017016540

Printed in the United States of America

To Our Readers: We have done our best to make sure all websites in this book were active and appropriate when we went to press. However, the author and the publisher have no control over and assume no liability for the material available on those websites or on any websites they may link to. Any comments or suggestions can be sent by email to customerservice@enslow.com.

Photo Credits: Cover Sergey Novikov/Shutterstock.com; p. 5 SolStock/E+/Getty Images; p. 6 Henn Photography/Cultura/Getty Images; p. 9 Ty Milford/Radius Images/Getty Images; p. 11 Lucky Business/Shutterstock.com; p. 14 Syda Productions/Shutterstock.com; p. 16 © iStockphoto.com/keithferrisphoto; pp. 20, 38 Hero Images/Getty Images; p. 23 Suzanne Tucker/Shutterstock.com; p. 24 Image Source/Getty Images; p. 28 Danil Nevsky /Shutterstock.com; pp. 31, 33 Westend61/Getty Images; p. 34 Patrik Giardino/Iconica /Getty Images; p. 41 Steven Errico/DigitalVision/Getty Images; cover and interior pages graphic elements © iStockphoto.com/marigold_88 (waves), Milos Djapovic/ Shutterstock.com (rough texture), Miloje/Shutterstock.com (circles).

CONTENTS

INTRODUCTION

There it is on your schedule. Maybe you should try to get out of it? But then again, it could be an easy A. Or … it could become a daily humiliation you are forced to endure. What if you don't know anyone? What if you can't keep up or remember the rules of a game?

Throughout this book, we'll take a look at what goes on in a typical gym class and show you how to prepare in advance so that the first day is more comfortable. Things have changed a lot over the years, and the gym class of the past is gone. You will learn about the new trend in PE, how the focus is now on health and well-being instead of fitness tests. We will discuss how getting a good night's rest and eating the proper food in advance of a workout is important. You will even learn how to master a few of the most dreaded gym traditions: the rope climb, the pull-up, and the 1-mile (1.6-kilometer) run.

There are things you need to know about navigating the locker room, and we'll share some tips so you can get back to class without the eau de gym attached to you—even without a shower. Even if the dreaded scenario happens and all your friends have a different schedule and you don't know anyone in your gym class, we'll show you how to make new friends. You will learn how to get through the tough

The gym class mile is usually the first race you'll ever run. With a little advance preparation, you can master it.

days, communicate effectively with your gym teacher, and get a good grade. There are a variety of situations that can come up in gym class, and after reading this book, you're going to be prepared to handle them.

You may need to unlearn some bad habits that many people tend to have, like negative self-talk. One of the worst

Don't isolate yourself! There's no reason to go it alone. Finding a friend in gym class can provide you with much needed support and encouragement.

things you can do is put yourself down. Saying things like "I can't do this," "I'm so uncoordinated," or "I'm not athletic at all" will only serve to make these insecure thoughts a reality—in your mind and in the minds of those around you. Because if you start gym class with the attitude that you can't or won't be able to succeed—there is a chance you won't.

You will learn that the key to success is centered on simply showing up, dressing out, and trying your very best. Unfortunately, there may be a time when you have to deal with a bully, a coach who yells at you in front of everyone, or making a mistake that loses the game. Fear not. We are going to help you deal with these situations and show you how to work through them and get past the tough spots.

OK. Deep breath, you've got this—or you will after reading this book. And surviving gym class is not the only goal—how about actually learning to enjoy it, look forward to it, and conquer it? Don't believe us? Well, we believe in you. You can do this!

CHAPTER ONE

DON'T DREAD IT

Let's begin with the basics.

WHAT HAPPENS IN GYM

You probably already know this, but let's go over it anyway. The gym itself will typically be a very large, open area with basketball hoops at either end (because it's also usually the same place your school hosts its basketball games). There may be banners on the wall if your school's sports teams have won any awards or recognition. There will probably be bleachers that fold away when gym class is in session. Many gyms also have a separate room where aerobics or other group classes can be held, and there may also be a weight room filled with various weight training equipment like barbells and other items.

While it can vary widely, the flow of a typical gym class is relatively similar at schools across the country. You will

Become familiar with the weight-training equipment at your school before gym class. Consider practicing at home or at your local gym first.

probably start out with stretching. A lot of times, this will lead to the dreaded warm-up run. Typically you will be asked to jog around a track outside or around the gym inside. This is usually followed up by the sport you are studying that week. Common sports are soccer, basketball, volleyball, badminton, tennis, flag football, and dodgeball.

YOU REALLY ARE WHAT YOU EAT

Your gym class might be first thing in the morning or the last part of the day. Regardless, you need the right fuel to power through with energy and alertness.

If you have a morning class, the meal to focus on is breakfast. Livestrong.com, a website about being healthy, explains that your overall performance depends on how you fuel up before a workout. So what food works the best? Bananas, almonds, yogurt with a little honey, eggs, peanut butter and crackers, or whole grain cereal and milk are easy and delicious options. If your class is in the afternoon, be careful about what you eat at lunch. That greasy slice of pizza might taste really good in the moment, but when you get to gym class, you will seriously wish you ate something else. Instead, pick lean proteins and whole grains, like a healthy turkey sandwich, which will keep your energy revved. Try to eat some carbohydrates—they will give you some quick energy and they digest rapidly, so they won't weigh you down. (A carbohydrate is a biological molecule. When it's broken down, it releases energy into your body. A protein is a nutrient found in food, made up of building blocks called amino acids. Proteins help your body function.)

Gauge your meal or snack by the type of activity you will be doing. According to Livestrong.com, intense cardiovascular workouts that will make you sweat and breathe heavily require

Eating healthy food can provide you with the energy and stamina you need to exercise at an optimal level.

more calories—aka extra food—while you'll need less for a lighter, shorter workout. And always drink plenty of water throughout the day. Sometimes when we feel slow and tired, it's because we simply haven't had enough water.

BEFORE YOU HIT THE GYM

Get proper sleep. We know, we know, you've heard it before, but it's true. You function better when you are well rested. Shoot for eight hours a night.

Don't skip breakfast. Have some whole wheat toast or a bagel with peanut butter. A little mix of carbohydrates and protein can give you the energy you need to feel good and energetic, according to Livestrong.com. Try to avoid too much sugar. It can give you an initial boost of energy—but the temporary effects quickly dissipate and often leave you feeling weak and tired.

GETTING YOUR MIND IN SHAPE

It's normal to feel nervous about something new and different. Change—whether it is good or bad—can be uncomfortable. Many students worry about gym class for all sorts of reasons. Maybe you don't consider yourself much of an athlete, or you are a little overweight—or underweight. Perhaps you don't have any friends in your gym class and you feel alone. While a little worry is normal and to be expected, if you let it get out of control it can really impact you negatively.

Therapist and health writer Mike Tyrrell says on the website uncommonhelp.me that he's convinced the mind is a powerful tool, and that it can work for or against you. When you spend a lot of time worrying about a situation, like being in gym class, you can end up being a lot more scared. Basically, the more you worry about something, the worse it seems.

Anxiety can then lead to panic each time you are in the situation you're stressing over. The solution lies in retraining your brain to feel calm and relaxed when you think of gym class. So take a few private moments every day to visualize your gym class in a calm, relaxed, and positive way. It may seem weird at first—and maybe a bit forced. But with regular commitment, you will find that your outlook and feelings about gym class begin to change, and you no longer immediately associate it with stress.

Tyrrell also advocates really noticing everything around you when you're in a situation that is making you very nervous. Notice everything: the color of the walls, the equipment, what is hanging on the walls, etc. Familiarity breeds comfort.

Your own imagination can also make you upset! We imagine everyone talking about us, thinking we're gross, or judging us. Tell your mind to be quiet when this begins to happen.

"Trying to imagine what people are thinking of you is a big no-no. Years of public speaking taught me to stop trying to gauge what others think of me," Tyrrell said. "So if you catch yourself 'mind-reading,' then tell yourself: 'Look, I really don't know what these other people are thinking right now!' because that's the truth of it. Ultimately we can influence what others think of us, but we can't control it. And as you become more socially confident, you'll care less anyway."

GET A WINNING ATTITUDE

"Ugh. We're running today? I'm not going to dress out!"

You may hear other kids say this a lot. You may even feel this way yourself. But the key to conquering gym class can be summed up in two words: Show up. That means attend class, dress out every day (no matter what), and follow instructions.

You might be surprised at how having a positive attitude, even when you might not really be feeling it, can lead to a happier and more optimistic mood.

If you Google "surviving gym class," thousands of videos will pop up. Most of them are created by people just like you. Many have experienced various difficulties in gym class—and they want to share what they know with you. Lots of kids are nervous about gym and know others are, too. It's important to remember you are not alone in this.

A lot of the same advice is shared again and again in various videos, and it basically comes down to the same thing: Show up. A huge part of succeeding in life is simply showing up. Even if you don't want to do the activity de jour, show up anyway. Knowing you are doing the right thing can have a hugely calming effect on your day.

CHAPTER TWO

ACE IT!

Sure, gym is a class, but guess what? It's a class where you don't have to be quiet or sit still! However, you do need to get to know your gym teacher. Understand what is important to them. How do they decide what grade you will get?

GET TO KNOW THE GYM TEACHER

The perception of gym teachers is often influenced by TV shows like "Glee," where the character Sue

Your gym teachers are not zany television characters, they're real human beings, with real emotions—and they are there to support you. Don't be afraid to talk to them.

Sylvester is merciless toward her students. We laugh as she treats them with cruelty and can't stop giggling when she unleashes an onslaught of insults. But it wouldn't be so funny if it really happened to us.

Believe it or not, teachers are people too. They were all once as young as you are—and they all had to survive gym class, too. A lot of times, gym teachers are well aware that there are students in their class who are less than thrilled to be there, and they really want to make you comfortable. Sometimes realizing your gym teacher is a human being, with all the emotions and experiences that come with that, makes it easier to feel you are in this together.

Take the example of teacher Nancy Flanagan. She taught classes in kindergarten through twelfth grade for thirty years and was named Michigan Teacher of the Year in 1993. When she was asked to take over a gym class for six weeks, it brought back memories, as she wrote about in a blog post for EdWeek.org.

"We wore hideous, balloon-butt red gym shorts and ugly white blouses, with snaps up the front and elastic hems for physical education classes," Flanagan said. "Simply putting them on was an exercise in humiliation."

When she was in middle school, her grade in gym class was based on performance. She and her classmates were required to run a fifty-yard (forty-five-meter) dash. When they finished, the gym teacher jotted down their time. They got to run it twice—and the best time became their grade.

HOW TO TALK TO ... DUN DUN DUN! ... YOUR GYM TEACHER

The first day of class, your teachers may let students know how to contact them. Listen and then follow through. If they don't tell you, ask. Approach your teacher when he or she doesn't look busy. Show up a little early for class, or stay a few minutes after class ends, and tell your teacher that you would like to set up a short time to chat about what to expect from gym class.

It might be a good idea to prepare a brief list of what you want to say and ask. It can be a little scary to meet with a teacher, and being nervous can easily cause you to completely forget everything you wanted to talk about.

Start off by saying that you want to succeed in gym class and would like to understand how you will be graded. This is how you'll find out what your teacher thinks—and what is important to him or her.

If you have any concerns, like an injury or disability—discuss it with the teacher now.

Ask your teacher to share an outline of the course, such as what sports you will be learning. This way, if you are unfamiliar with some of them, you have time to learn more and practice a bit on your own so you can come to class prepared.

Not being an athlete, her poor grade in gym class actually kept her off the honor roll. But her personal experiences had an effect on the way she chose to teach gym class when it was her turn many years later. And in her gym class, everyone who tried received an A.

The key word here is "tried."

Showing your interest in gym and displaying a willingness to try each sport will score high marks with a teacher like Nancy Flanagan. Meanwhile, slacking off, complaining, and not dressing out could result in a failing grade. The lesson here is that it's important to know what kind of teacher you have and what is important to them in the grading process. Don't assume. Talk to them.

CHANGES IN PE

While some gym teachers give more performance-based grades, across the country the trend in physical education classes is changing. Now it is more about fitness, education, and learning healthy habits. This is different from testing how fast or far you can run, jump, and more, which is how things used to be.

"People see the physical education teachers as the guy who tortures them to see how many push-ups they can do in a minute," said Cheryl L. Richardson, senior director of programs for the Society of Health and Physical Educators.

It takes time to build up your fitness level. It feels great when you improve your running time or increase the number of reps you can do. It means your body is getting healthier and stronger!

"PE teachers today have much higher expectations. It's more of a learning environment. We want kids to learn about their own personal fitness and to make decisions about that."

In 2012, the President's Fitness Challenge, an American program created to encourage all Americans to become active, and its youth physical fitness testing curriculum got a major makeover. It was renamed the Presidential Youth Fitness Program and the emphasis was changed from a focus on the results of physical challenges (like how fast you can run or how high you can jump) and replaced with a move toward teaching fitness for life, health, and personal well-being.

Approximately twenty-five thousand schools, with an estimated reach of thirteen million students (that's a lot!), are engaged with the Presidential Youth Fitness Program—so maybe that includes you and your gym class.

Still, many school districts let their teachers decide how to organize and run their gym class—and how grades will be decided. In states like Florida, teacher's evaluations (yes, teachers get graded too!) and how much money they make is linked to how well their students do on PE tests. No wonder they want you to do well!

If your gym class teacher will give you your grade based on the results of performance tests, like how fast you run and how many push-ups you can do, it's important to know at the beginning of the year. Talk to your teacher about any worries you have and ask him or her for advice so you can earn the best grade possible.

CHAPTER THREE

YOU'RE NOT ALONE

In gym class, try to give off an air of self-confidence, like you know what you're doing— even if you don't completely feel like you do. It will come eventually. Just as we talked about training your brain to relax and release worry and anxiety, you can also train yourself to feel confidence by simply believing you are confident. In other words, fake it till you make it.

DON'T SLOUCH!

Do your best in class. Don't slouch, don't sit down first. Instead, stretch out and keep your eyes up. Make eye contact when spoken to. Don't stare at the ground. Put away your cell phone. You don't want to look uncomfortable or uninvolved. If you are supposed to run, don't walk every time the gym teacher looks away. They might not see, but other people will. Instead, try your best. You just might find that soon the others in class who want to try hard will start hanging out with you.

The number one thing you can do to improve your success in gym class is to show up with a positive attitude.

DON'T SWEAT THE "OTHERS"

It can sometimes seem like there's a group of kids in every class who think it's cool to look down on others. You know, they're the people who rarely dress out and can often be found in the bleachers staring, pointing, and giggling at those who are participating and enjoying the activity. Ignore them. If someone happens to single you out, and you feel bullied, HelpGuide.org suggests a few effective ways to deal with it. First, try not to be alone. Hang out

Avoiding conflict can be tricky but it's all about learning to keep your cool while having the courage to stand up for yourself. Bullies thrive on fear. Don't be afraid. And reach out to an adult if you need extra help.

with your friends as much as you can. If the bully gets in your face, face him or her directly without emotion and tell the person to stop. Don't let the bully see that you are upset—that's exactly what bullies want. Walk away. Also, and this is really important, don't ever tolerate physical violence. Report it immediately. Confide in a trusted adult. Believe it or not, bullying behavior comes from a place of insecurity. Keep that in mind if someone is giving you a difficult time. The bully feels unsure and uncomfortable and he or she is acting out. And it is not okay. You are dealing with an insecure person who lacks basic social skills and probably has an unhappy life. Don't let the bully affect your life and your happiness.

LEAN ON ME

Sometimes none of your friends will be in the same gym class. It happens. Don't panic. There are a lot of other students in your class who probably have the same issue, which means it's the perfect opportunity to make new friends. Everyone feels better with a friend nearby. You can cheer each other on, laugh, and learn.

How do you make a friend? Get out of your head and infuse yourself with confidence. Compliment the accomplishments of others. Introduce yourself, start a conversation. Ask them for help with a machine or go on a warm-up run together.

GETTING THROUGH A BAD DAY

We all have them. The crummy days we just don't feel motivated. Maybe it's because of a recent breakup, a fight with your parent, or just a case of the sads that suddenly hits.

Sometimes it starts with something like forgetting to set your alarm and waking up late. Then you trip on your way to the bathroom and hurt your knee, you miss your first class and get in trouble with the teacher and all you want to do is go home, get under the covers, and hide.

In her article "Having a Bad Day" on the website VeryWell .com, writer Elizabeth Scott explains that often "a day that starts out bad just keeps getting worse, snowballing into a really bad day." She calls this the domino effect, and if you don't get control of it quickly, the day can spiral into a really, really bad day.

To counteract the domino effect, she suggests trying the "locus of control." Scott says "it has to do with whether or not you view your situation as a 'threat' or as a 'challenge.' It may seem clear-cut which you're experiencing, but a mild shift in how you view things can actually help you go from feeling trapped and overwhelmed to feeling invigorated and vital." Basically the locus of control is the belief that you control your own destiny, instead of thinking that outside events control you.

To use the technique, remember these tips. You have a choice. You can change your situation, even if it is just your attitude. Take a moment to review your options. Make a quick mental or written list of the ways you can change the mood of the day. Forget phrases like "I can't" and "I have no choice." No more negative self-talk.

You may not be able to change a situation, but you can change your attitude toward it. And your attitude can have a major effect on your stress levels.

HANDLING HOOTING AND HOLLERING

So we know that teachers are human beings complete with emotions. It would be unrealistic to assume they are always in control of those emotions; we all lose it once in a while, right? Your gym teacher might get angry—and may even yell—at you. How are you going to handle it? Here are some tips. There's even a wiki online called, "How Not to Cry When a Teacher Yells at You," so you're not the only one this has happened to.

First, try to stay calm. If you feel tears beginning to form, politely ask to be excused to the bathroom for a moment. If you can't leave, try to refocus your mind and think of something

(continued on the next page)

(continued from the previous page)

else. Concentrate on your breathing. Take some deep breaths. Sometimes counting objects in your head works or squeezing the bridge of your nose. Resist the urge to yell back. Stay quiet and calm. After you've had a chance to recover, try to schedule a private chat with your teacher. If you've done something wrong, tell the teacher you will commit to doing better. However, if there are frequent episodes involving you, it's probably time to reach out to the school counselor or a parent for an effective solution.

There may come a time when you get in trouble with a gym teacher. Remain calm, listen, and try not to get too emotional. Everyone has a bad day once in a while.

PUSH IT

The good news is that physical activity can really help reduce stress. Exercise releases a flood of feel-good endorphins into the brain. It literally helps you blow off steam. So look at your gym class as a chance to push the negative energy out of your body and mind.

There will be days you are tired, have cramps, feel bloated, forgot to shave your legs, left your "good" underwear at home, or neglected to wash your uniform. The key on these days is just to show up, dress out, and get it done. Everyone has gone through the same thing.

Take things one day at a time, one friendship at a time, and don't get caught up in drama and gossip. Tough times always pass, so look forward. Get a good night's sleep. Don't be too hard on yourself. It's OK to be who you are. Challenge yourself and take advantage of new opportunities but don't get down on yourself if it doesn't work out like you hoped it would. There's always tomorrow.

CHAPTER FOUR

CONQUERING THE LOCKER ROOM

HAVE THE RIGHT GEAR

Having the right outfit can help boost your confidence and get you on your way to kicking butt in gym class. Get a good pair of gym shoes and the right socks. Keep your laces tight.

Bring water, deodorant, hair ties if you need them, and a change of clothes.

If your school requires a uniform, think about buying two so it's easier to always have a clean one on hand. You will need to wash your uniform after almost every gym class—even if it's just a quick dunk in the sink with laundry detergent and water.

Have a large ziplock or separate bag to keep your used gym clothes away from everything else in your backpack so you can bring your clothes home to wash without stinking up the rest of your stuff.

If you are able to use the gym lockers, buy a lock if your school doesn't provide one and write the combo with a marker underneath the tongue of your gym shoe.

SHOE 411

The most economical choice in gym shoes are cross-trainers, according to LiveStrong.com. They provide good cushioning for comfort and stability. The soles have the right amount of traction to provide support for a bunch of different sports and are thick enough to perform well on indoor gym floors as well as concrete.

It's very important to select the right size shoes for you. If they are too tight, your feet will hurt and you could get painful

(continued on the next page)

The right gym shoes can make all the difference. Try on a few pairs to see what feels best—and be sure to get the right size for your foot.

(continued from the previous page)

blisters that keep you from participating in class. If they are too large, you could easily trip or they could fall off in the middle of a game. Try on a few pairs in different sizes. Different manufacturers often have a different fit. If you buy them online, make sure there is a refund policy, or try them on at a local store first.

Get the right socks, too. Make sure they fit comfortably, and wear them when you try on your shoes. Try to buy a large amount of socks, wash them all together, and keep them in their own drawer for easy retrieval.

Flat shoes like Converse Chuck Taylors may be stylish, but they are not for gym class. The flat, stiff sole can be uncomfortable—and make you more likely to hurt yourself. So save them for another time—outside of gym class.

A LESSON IN STINK

The majority of school-issued gym clothes are made from polyester. This fabric keeps you dry and cool and wicks away sweat during a workout. But they can also work up a stink after sitting in your locker.

According to Amanda L. Chan, who wrote the article "Why You Should Wash Those Dirty Gym Clothes Immediately," for the *Huffington Post* website, that's because odor-causing bacteria, called micrococci, appear to thrive

Since you might not have time to shower, keep your gym shoes smelling fresh simply by remembering to wear a good pair of clean socks.

and grow on polyester more than they do on cotton.

You may be surprised to know that sweat itself doesn't smell. However the micrococci can turn sweat secretions smelly.

So the bottom line is: wash your uniform on a regular basis. Even though it may not smell when you take it off right after gym, it will most likely stink to high heaven after twenty-four hours in your locker.

THE QUICK CHANGE

You will probably be changing in front of everyone. Most people find a locker and base themselves there—facing the locker while changing. Don't feel embarrassed. Everyone is in the same situation. For the girls, consider wearing a bra, even if you don't need one, if you don't want to have your

Changing in the locker room may take some getting used to. Just remember that everyone else feels the same way you do, and no one is focusing on anyone but themselves.

naked chest out in front of others. You can get a workout bra, tank top, or even an undershirt. Think about what would be most comfortable for you and go for it. For guys and girls, always wear clean underwear you feel comfortable in.

You will find that other students may not use the showers. If no one else is using them, you might not want to be the only one who does. Bring some soap for a quick sink bath or keep a stash of baby wipes on hand for a quick refresh.

A WORD ABOUT BULLIES

The locker room is one of the most vulnerable places you can be in school. People are undressing, underwear is on display, and you're trying to bathe in a sink. It can be a prime spot for someone to try to embarrass or humiliate you with a comment or worse. With no adult supervision in sight, it can be a real issue if someone decides to bother you in the locker room. Don't stand for it. Report it immediately. School administrators take bullying very seriously and can deal with the bully effectively so that he or she doesn't bother anyone else. Don't ever be afraid to stand up for yourself or what's right.

PREVENTING INFECTION

Fungus feels right at home in warm, dark places. Locker rooms can be ripe locations for all the nasties that cause infection. To stay healthy, keep your hands clean, wash them often with soap, or use a hand sanitizer with at least 60 percent alcohol content. That's what the Centers for Disease Control and Prevention recommends.

If you can, buy a cheap pair of flip-flops and wear them in the locker room instead of walking around in your bare feet. That way you won't pick up a case of athlete's foot.

Don't share towels or gym clothes; you could also be sharing bacteria. And if you get a cut, tell the teacher you need antibacterial cream and a Band-Aid—items usually kept in a first-aid kit that should be on hand.

The more you're prepared for gym class, the easier it will be! We promise.

CHAPTER FIVE

DON'T KNOW IT? LEARN IT!

The other kids in your gym class come from all kinds of athletic backgrounds and experiences. Some have played on recreational or competitive sports teams since they were very young, others have exercised occasionally or played a round of basketball for fun every once in a while—and some emphatically despise exercise or sports of any kind.

Even if athletics isn't your thing, you have to come to grips with the fact that it is now, indeed, your thing. You need to take gym class, and since it's one of those things you have to do, why not make it the best experience it can be?

Much of the fear related to gym comes from the unknown. So let's take a look at what might go on in your class, so you'll know what to expect, and then come up with a plan to succeed.

GET YOUR FITNESS ON

First, don't let PE class be the only time you work out. Find some physical activities you enjoy doing. You may go through some trial and error before you discover what motivates you to exercise, but in time, it will come.

There are so many choices, from swimming, hiking, surfing, and cycling to jumping rope, Zumba (an aerobic fitness class infused with Latin dance moves and music), yoga, and kayaking. Mix it up and make it fun. Bring a friend along. Having company can go a long way to making exercising a good time.

Exercising outside of school hours is a great way to get fit and have fun. Try some new activities with a few friends. You might surprise yourself by realizing you enjoy working out!

Go to the park and walk or jog. Start small and gradually go farther and faster. With regular exercise, it won't be so hard to run that mile in gym.

Find a place where you can practice on the equipment you might find in class. Many parks have workout trails with rope climbs and pull-up bars. Give them a go. Once you get to gym, your body won't feel so clunky because you have practiced on your own.

Get to know the machines in the weight room if your school has one. You might consider joining a local gym. Ask a trainer to explain the workout equipment. Have the trainer show you how to properly use it. Once you know what you are doing, people may start to approach you for advice. Become a leader.

TACKLING TOUGH OBSTACLES

How to Climb a Knotted Rope

We checked out an article on rope climbing by Margaret Schlachter on the website Fitness Rx for Women to get you some pointers on this gym-class staple. It can seem tough to tackle, but with the right info, we know you can do it!

1. Grab the rope with both hands above the highest knot possible.

(continued on the next page)

(continued from the previous page)

2. Pull down on the rope while jumping a bit to lift yourself into the air.
3. Reach up as high as you can with your arms and grip the rope tightly.
4. Using your core (abdominal muscles) bring your knees up to your chest, finding the highest comfortable knot with your feet.
5. Pinch the arches of your shoes around the knot to cup it and give you a platform to stand on.
6. Stand up with your legs and re-reach as high as possible with your arms.
7. Repeat steps four through seven until you reach the top of the rope. In many races, you will ring a bell at the top.
8. Use the knots to climb down. Lower your body knot by knot. If you are afraid of heights, you can sit on the knots as you lower yourself down.

How to Do a Pull-Up

The key to being able to do a pull-up is achieving back and arm strength. Try the following exercises from the Nerd Fitness website, focusing on lifting more and more as you get stronger: Every other day, pick up a dumbbell that you can lift for three sets of eight repetitions, with a two-minute break between sets. As soon as you can do three sets of eight reps, it's time to move up to a heavier dumbbell.

Body weight rows are another good exercise before trying pull ups: they work the same muscles, just at a different angle. Bodyweight exercises are strength training exercises that do not require free weights or machines because you use your own weight as resistance. This exercise has been referred to as the reverse bench press. You grab a bar as if getting ready to bench press it, but instead of lifting the weight down toward you, you're pulling your body up toward the bar.

Start with a higher bar at first then lower it gradually. You can find bars on fitness trails in many parks or at local schools.

Nervous about an upcoming activity in gym class? Practice it on your own time so you're more comfortable when it's time to do it in front of the whole class.

TAKE A RISK

Here's some advice you may not want to hear but we're going to share it anyway. Even if you hate gym, consider trying out for the toughest sport that is the least like you. It takes guts, and it may feel awkward, but there is a reason this is a good idea.

The process of trying out for a team usually takes a few days, sometimes even a few weeks. During this time, you have the chance to get to know some new people, and it's easy to form a bond when you have a common goal. You may not make the team the first year you try out, or ever for that matter, but if you consider that fifty people may try out and only fifteen make the team, that means there are thirty-five students who also didn't make it. This creates a pool of kids you can connect with. Start your own recreational team and play the sport together. You can learn together and make friends. You may have played basketball your whole life, but why not give soccer a try? Sometimes we stick with the thing we are comfortable with and don't give ourselves the chance to discover new sports we may love. If you are too afraid to try you never will realize you really love weight lifting or crew or tennis or … who knows?! Try it. You may like it.

Attend games at your school, too. It's a great way to learn a sport you don't know—and there's no risk involved. This way, when it's time to play this sport in gym class, or another activity you've never tried, you'll feel more confident because you'll know there's no harm in trying and failing. All that matters is the effort you put in and (if you're lucky!) the fun you'll have.

SURVIVING THE MISTAKE THAT LOST THE GAME

If you make an error during a game in gym class that results in a loss, it can be hard to deal with, but you are in good company. There are thousands of professional athletes who share the experience of making a game-losing mistake. So, first things first, let's put it in perspective. This is gym class, not the World Series, like when Bill Buckner let an easy ground ball roll through his legs, making him a national scapegoat for causing the historic loss.

In his article "How Athletes Deal with Being the Goat That Lost the Game," writer Kevin L. Burke says on SportingNews .com that it's important to remember a game is not won or lost on one play. In a typical football game there are 150 plays, and there are double that amount in basketball. Over the course of a game, numerous mistakes are commonly made by players, coaches, and even referees.

But the best advice he offers athletes who have made a mistake is this: "Its history." So forget it, and move on.

IN A NUTSHELL

You will survive this. We think you will even look back on it and smile.

Just remember to always keep your sense of humor. Embrace the benefits of physical fitness, how it improves your mood and makes you stronger and more confident. Learn new things, embrace new opportunities and friendships. Set personal goals. Don't let a bad day pull you down. Shrug off your inner critic, and quiet the negative self-talk. Don't insult yourself. Believe in yourself.

Now go to gym class. You got this. Believe it.

GLOSSARY

assertiveness The ability to express your ideas without hesitation.

bacteria One-celled organisms that can cause disease.

carbohydrate A biological molecule consisting of carbon, hydrogen, and oxygen atoms. When broken down, it releases energy in the body.

competitive team A team based on winning matches and ranking high. Made up of more experienced players.

economical Being of a good value in relation to the money spent.

endurance The level of ability a person shows to commit to and complete something difficult.

profound Meaningful in an intense way.

recreational team A team based around having fun and learning a sport better. Made up of less experienced players.

resilience The ability to bounce back after something challenging.

revved Excited; used to describe how you feel about something you are looking forward to.

scapegoat Someone who is blamed for causing something bad, though they are often not the actual cause.

syllabus A document typically handed out to students on the first day of class that outlines the teacher's expectations of the students, usually including homework and reading assignments.

Zumba An aerobic fitness class infused with Latin dance moves and music.

FURTHER READING

BOOKS

Brezina, Corona. *Helping a Friend Who Is Being Bullied*. New York, NY: Rosen Publishing, 2017.

Covey, Sean. *The 7 Habits of Highly Effective Teens*. New York, NY: Touchstone, 2014.

Daniels, Natasha. *Anxiety Sucks! A Teen Survival Guide*. Seattle, WA: Create Space Publishing, 2016.

Rissman, Rebecca. *Yoga for Your Mind and Body: A Teenage Practice for a Healthy, Balanced Life*. North Mankato, MN: Capstone Press, 2015.

WEBSITES

I Am Beautiful

iambeautiful.org

This award-winning nonprofit organization engages girls in interactive learning experiences designed to build self-esteem and strong leadership skills to help girls and women live beautiful lives inside and out.

Kids.gov

kids.usa.gov/teens/exercise-fitness-nutrition/index.shtml

The official kids' portal for the US government, this site offers a variety of information on healthy eating with fun recipes and advice on diet, exercise, and sports.

La Belle Foundation

selfesteem.org

Founded in 1980, this nonprofit's objective is to bring the teaching of self-esteem, self-development, and personal and social responsibility to public school students.

INDEX